American History

US History: An Overview of the Most Important People & Events. The History of United States: From Indians to Contemporary History of America

not engaging in the rendering of legal, financial, medical or professional advice.

By reading this document, the reader agrees that under no circumstances are we responsible for any losses, direct or indirect, which are incurred as a result of the use of information contained within this document, including, but not limited to, —errors, omissions, or inaccuracies.

Table of Contents

Introduction

The United States of America is one, if not the most powerful country in the whole world. However, it was not always like this. Throughout its long and illustrious history, the USA has gone through a rollercoaster of events. Quite a number of wrong choices and misunderstandings have almost torn the country apart, but there were also quite a lot of things that happened that made the USA stronger than ever.

In this book, you will learn about some of the most significant events in US History. Hopefully, by the end of the book, you'd learn enough about the colorful history of the United States that it would rekindle a newfound sense of interest within you.

Chapter 1 – Pre-Colonial Times, Christopher Columbus, and the Accidental Discovery of America

Many people tend to think of the beginning of America as starting with Christopher Columbus, and while this certainly rings true for a number of reasons, the fact of the matter is that there were people living in North America long before he arrived. Most Native Americans and Paleolithic peoples were hunter gatherers, and there have been artifacts found that date to almost 14,000 BC, indicating that there were thriving cultures here for several millennia. Some of the earliest societies would have included the Adena People and the Mississippian People who built raised cities and were likely one of the first North Americans to adopt an agrarian style of living, growing and harvesting maize. Other crops included berries, potatoes, tomatoes, squash, and beans.

Later on the Iroquois people also inhabited the land that would one day become the pre United States, and were actually quite advanced. They produced a democratic society that many theorists believe actually helped to inspire the eventual writing of the United States Constitution. Evidence of their civilization has more or less vanished in a physical sense, but the legends and mythology they left behind is still a subtle influence in the makeup of the United States.

The first European to come to the Americas *was* in fact Christopher Columbus. There were a number of prior missions that failed to reach America, but Columbus was determined. He was an Italian-born explorer who had been traveling the vast oceans under the name of the Portuguese Crown. During his time, the Portuguese were one of the strongest countries in the world, thanks in part to their numerous trade ships and trade agreements with many countries in Africa and some parts of India.

During Columbus's time, many people still believed that the earth was flat and that if you sailed too far, you risk falling off the edge and into oblivion. Columbus did not really subscribe to the theory of a flat earth, thanks mostly to the invention of the printing press and the distribution of scholarly articles between countries. However, he wasn't a sole proponent of the idea of a round earth either. Rather, he was under the impression that the earth was shaped somewhat like a pear, with an oblong dimension to it.

At the time, the only way for merchant ships to reach Asia was by following the African coast and crossing the Indian Ocean, which was quite a long and terrifying journey. Columbus believed that it would be faster, and much safer to sail westward and cross the Pacific and into the continent of Asia. Not only would this assumedly cut down on the dangerous and costly sailing time, but it would create a corridor to the Asian markets that would, Columbus hoped, benefit Portugal. Unfortunately, the king of Portugal did not intend to let Columbus take a fleet of his ships over the edge of the world.

This setback did not deter Columbus in the least. When the Portuguese crown did not let him circumnavigate the earth, he cut his ties with the crown and went to other countries to offer his services. Columbus went to England and France, and he pitched his idea of establishing a shorter trade route so they can gain access to the riches of Asia. However, both the English and French monarchs also believed that the earth was flat and that his plan was pure folly. However, in 1492, King Ferdinand and Queen Isabela of Spain somehow got interested in Columbus's proposition and agreed to finance his "crazy" expeditions.

On August 3, 1492, Christopher Columbus took his three ships, the Pinta, the Niña, and the Santa Maria, out of the Spanish port town of Palos and sailed westward. Understandably, Columbus's crew did not share his beliefs, and they are all terrified at the prospect of sailing over the edge of the world. To appease his crewmembers, Columbus kept two logbooks; one contained the real distance that they have travelled, and a second one that shows a considerably lesser amount. He kept the first book a secret from the crew. However, the crew started to become suspicious about their travels.

To stop his crew from committing mutiny in the high seas, Columbus made a promise that if by two days they still haven't found land, they will turn around and head back home to Spain. As luck would have it, they found land the next day.

On October 12, 1492, Columbus landed in what he believed to be India, but what was actually a South American island, which he named Hispaniola (this island is now a part of the Dominican Republic).

Did Columbus even land in North America?

Unfortunately, Columbus never even set foot in North America. Rather, he ended up landing on a number of the Caribbean Islands and made several voyages that ended up reaching South America. However, he did establish a safer route for ships to get to the Americas, and this paved the way for other explorers to make their way into North America and what would eventually become the United States. Although Columbus was preceded by a number of much earlier nautical ventures by Vikings like Leif Erikson, who *would* have reached the North American continent, Columbus' influence – especially on the indigenous populations – was markedly more significant, and laid the foundation for centuries of exploitation and colonial expansion, something is still felt even today by North America's surviving modern indigenous peoples. At the time, Portuguese and Spanish society was heavily influenced by the effects and ubiquity of Christian theology, and this extended to the notion that it was important and imperative to spread religious beliefs to as many corners of the globe as possible. However, whatever the intentions of devout missionaries, this attempt at re-culturation ended up having a much more negative impact. Many missionaries were killed, but many more natives were massacred by conquistadors attempting to supplant the endemic spiritual beliefs of South American peoples.

The irony of Columbus' blunder in the South America was compounded by the fact that, even until his death in 1506, he was a stout believer that he had actually found a way to the East Indies and refused to believe that he had landed on a separate hereto unknown body of land. This can be traced back to the etymological and linguistic origins for why, up until very recently, North American's indigenous people were called "Indians" – Columbus believed wholeheartedly that he had actually reached India.

Chapter 2 – The Early Settlers

After the news of a new route across the Atlantic had reached Europe, there was a flurry of interest. The Spanish and Portuguese set off to conquer large areas of South and Central America over the centuries, building huge overseas empires that flooded them their economies with goods and materials. Spain is even said to have imported so much gold that the value of it decreased significantly across Europe; this sudden and huge spike in the supply of gold may have caused economic problems for the monarchy and subsequently destroyed the Spanish empire. The Europeans encountered countless Native American tribes and even some empires. As we know today, these Native American empires eventually succumbed to Spanish and Portuguese military powers largely thought amplified greatly by no immunity to Old World diseases. The Aztecs, Mayans, and Incas are the well-known empires we have all learned about in history class.

This book, however, does not focus on those areas of the world. What was happening in North America? As the Spanish were early to the game, they founded a colony in Florida in 1560 and even before that they were exploring areas now included in the United States. Twenty years before their Florida colony, the Spanish observed and explored the California coast. But these events are tangential to US American history. What was happening in Florida and California were of significantly less relevance than what happened just a few decades later.

Spain wanted to invade the English mainland, and they had the naval firepower to launch an attack. However, the attack failed when the English destroyed the Spanish Armada in 1588. The English themselves wanted a piece of the new world, and in 1607, they had already set up a colony at Jamestown. The main drivers for this interest in the New World were economic, though religion and national rivalry in Europe also played major roles in the expansion of European empires over the next four centuries.

The English were surprisingly late to establish colonies, as France, Spain, and Portugal happily explored and staked out claims in the newfound world quickly following Columbus' discovery. Many of the early English colonies were failures, but fate turned a smile towards them eventually, as the United States is a descendant not of Portuguese, French, or Spanish but of the English. Following the mysterious disappearance of the Roanoke colony in 1590, the English finally set up Jamestown, and the colony became a success.

JAMESTOWN

This colony was set up in what would become the US State of Virginia in 1607. The state is named after the company that settled the area, The Virginia Company. Most ventures were set up as companies, as this was, first and foremost, an economic expedition to capitalize on the New World's opportunities. And the Virginia Company was no different. Their goal? To mine gold and silver from the New World for the glory of England. They also wanted to find a trade route across the newly discovered North American Continent in hopes of trading with the highly lucrative Orient – the original plan of Christopher Columbus.

The commander of the voyage left in summer 1607 to report the new settlement's findings and location to the monarchy in England. Those left behind struggled to survive in the New World where they faced not only disease and famine but also attacks from the local Native American tribes who were loosely organized by the Chief Powhatan. The conflict between the new settlers and the Natives eventually subsided to just a few skirmishes here and there. The settlers established trade, which helped them subsist through the early years. The most common types of trades included beads and metal tools (including weapons) for foodstuffs.

After multiple setbacks and a brutal winter which killed a large number of settlers, the colony was set to be abandoned, just like the other English colonies before it. However, two ships arrived from England right before abandonment, which bore at least 150 new people to settle, supplies to help the colony survive, and, perhaps most importantly, a newly appointed governor of the colony. A ragtag group of settlers cannot survive without some sort of leadership.

The settlers had learned much from the local Algonquin tribe. The English started to build forts along the James River, and in 1611 they had harvested their own corn successfully. The relative peace between the settlers and Algonquins did not last, and even though the settlers had learned and prospered thanks to the Natives, they had started to raid their villages and kill their members. The marriage between a settler and a Native (John Smith and Pocahontas), the peace returned.

As this was an economic venture, it began to really thrive after the introduction of a strain of tobacco that could grow in the region. The beginnings of the democratic process (for male landowners, at least) was set up in the region, and eventually, Africans were brought to the Americas; the origins of slavery in America had sprouted.

PLYMOUTH COLONY

A different type of colony was set up further north in what would become Massachusetts. In late 1620 three ships arrived on the New England coast to form a new settlement. The ships were two months late, and December is not a good month to start a new colony. The winter was brutal, and half of the original settlers died in the first winter. The remainder was able to form peace with the local tribes and established themselves as another success in English colonial history within the next five years.

Nearly half of the settlers were Pilgrims. They were seeking not only economic opportunities but also religious freedom.

They were Puritans who had extreme interpretations of the Protestant Reformation and did not believe the Anglican Church was fulfilling the requirements. They had tried staying in Europe in the Netherlands, a notoriously tolerant country, but did not want to lose their English language and heritage. Hence they set out to the New World, which offered a place to practice their radical beliefs.

One of the most famous incidents of Protestant migration was the eminent *Mayflower*. This ship landed in 1620 and contained primarily Protestants that were trying to escape religious persecution back in England. It has gone down in history as one of the premiere examples of both immigration into the United States, and conversely an example of how hard it was to survive in the New World, whose harsh climate and terrifying winters were an unexpected disaster for many. Many of the original pilgrims faced not only the danger of weather, but also attack from animals, hypothermia and illnesses, and accidents.

The colonists developed relations with a single Native American who had previously been captured and taken to England. He managed to escape back to North America, and he was able to liaise between the new colonists and the local tribe already present. The colonists and Natives shared a harvest feast together in 1621, which became the US American holiday of Thanksgiving. The colonists had survived largely due to help from the Natives, and the success likely reinforced their notions of being God-sent.

Other colonies sprung up along the coast which had similar guiding principles, but these eventually became economical in nature. Religious considerations were not fully abandoned, but commerce became the most important driving force. Of course, this meant a hunger for more land and power, which resulted in conflict with the Natives. Intermittent violence occurred and culminated in a full war in 1675 (King Philip's War of 1675). The power and influence of Plymouth started to fade as other, more successful colonies forged ahead, and the colony was absorbed by Massachusetts by the end of the 17th century.

CALIFORNIA COLONIES

While the European influx into the New World was rampant, the Spanish and Portuguese were no slouches either. Capitalizing on the foothold they had made in earlier sailing voyages and cemented by Columbus' first visit, a number of ships cruised up and down the Californian coast, but very few if any colonies were established between the 16th and 18th centuries. However, a number of soldiers and priests did explore this area greatly, and helped to build *presidos* or religious monasteries and missions that were inhabited primarily by Franciscan monks. One of the first was established by Father Junipero Serra called the Mission San Diego de Alcala in 1769, and represented a concerted effort by the Spanish to continue their proselytization of the West into the Christian faith.

NEW FRANCE

The French were not prepared to lose out on the early land claims that would one day shape North America into its present incarnation, and were also heavily involved in a number of expeditions that established 'New France', an area consisting of present day Acadia, Newfoundland, Mississippi, and various islands in the Canadian peninsula (including Cape Breton Island and Prince Edward Island). In the early to late 1600's there was a huge and booming industry of fur trappers extending all the way down the coast and was extremely profitable to the motherland of France back home. It wasn't until the War for Independence in 1783 that much of the land beneath the Great Lakes area became part of the United States, and by then there were already a number of French colonies with thriving populations, including Illinois Country that sported nearly 2,500 people.

Additionally, French Louisiana was also a lucrative stretch of land, reaching from the Midwest and the Rockies all the way to upper and lower Louisiana. In 1700 several colonies sprung up at Mobile and Biloxi, and it would be only a matter of years before a huge party of French migrants – nearly 7000 in total – would found the iconic city of New Orleans in 1718. Situated on the banks of the Mississippi, it would act as a major transportation and commerce hub, and though the development and expansion of New Orleans was slow to start, its value as an economic powerhouse was undisputed.

Several decades later the grip that France had in the Americas would start to decline when, in 1763, it would begin to cede several territories in and around Mississippi and New Orleans back to France. In a way, this marked the beginning of the end for France's control of its colonial powers, and would eventually culminate with the 1803 watershed event of the Louisiana Purchase.

Chapter 3 – The Formation of the 13 Colonies

As mentioned, most of these colonies were developed for economic reasons. The population of England was growing, and the gigantic landmass of North America provided an outlet for those people. The prevailing economic model at the time, mercantilism, drove the European powers into competition in an effort to gather more power and prestigious than the neighbors.

Mercantilism attempted to magnify state power by increasing economic power (something that really has never disappeared). The National government would regulate trade in an attempt to achieve a positive balance of trade, especially for finished goods. The New World could supply a huge amount of natural resources (as Spain and Portugal had done with gold and silver) and hence mercantilism drove colonialism. Furthermore, the government regulation sometimes included a prohibition on trading with other colonies. This style of economic activity frequently led to war, and many wars throughout European and early American history have an economic conflict as a basis.

A competitor to Virginia, Maryland, was granted in 1632. The grant from the English Crown was for 12 million acres of land, and the colony relied heavily on a single cash crop for its prosperity. The colony, however, was intended to be Catholic and a refuge for persecuted Catholics in Anglican England; the colony became known for its religious freedom, a departure from some of the colonies further north (such as Massachusetts and Connecticut). It was less religiously permissive than Rhode Island, though.

The main export of Virginia and Maryland was tobacco, which was shipping back to Europe. The plant had been first introduced by Native Americans, and the Europeans quickly took to smoking the substance. One of the two major crops that supported the southern colonies on the East Coast, it became an essential export for the American colonies. Cotton would become the other major cash crop for the southern colonies, as the developing Industrial Revolution in England demanded raw materials for its factories. These factories turned out finished goods (textiles), augmenting the power of the English Crown.

New York (City) was established as English while many settlers from other regions (including Germans, Scandinavians, Frenchmen, and Belgians) stayed in the area. Pennsylvania was established as a relatively religiously tolerant colony that also prospered, as many of its residents were able to support themselves once they arrived in the colony.

The Carolina Colony was not so diverse. In the northern areas it contained subsistence farmers and in the south, it was largely planters who made money from cash crops such as corn and rice, plus livestock. The southern plantation output was made possible by slave labor, and many of the planters were themselves in the business. The Carolina Colony was also huge, with its charter giving it reign over everything south of Virginia to Spain-controlled Florida with a breadth stretching all the way to the Pacific Ocean. However, in 1732, in order to protect the increasing importance of Carolina, Georgia was established as a buffer colony between the English colonies and Spanish Florida.

From the meager settlements of early 1600 with a few hundred colonists, in 1700 the population of the Thirteen Colonies is estimated at about 250,000. Over the next three-quarters of a century, the population exploded, driven by natural births and immigration of people from all over Europe into the colonies. The colonies offered economic and religious opportunities for many escaping the Old World. In the next 75 years, the population multiplied itself by nearly 100, boasting a population of 2.5 million at the time of the American Revolution. As a comparison, the population in the controlling

England in 1700 was about 5.2 million and by the time of the American Revolution, it had risen to around 7 million. The population grew much more rapidly in the colonies, but the British Isles are tiny in comparison to the vast area the Thirteen Colonies covered. It is also easier for a small population to achieve faster growth rates as raw numbers do not have to be so great.

The colonies were largely still part of English culture and society, and the sparks that caused the American Revolution largely centered around the disagreement between who should control politics. As is known by every student of American History, a major point of consternation was taxation of colonial wealth by the Crown. England, following the ideas of mercantilism, surely wanted to increase governmental power by increasing wealth. The Crown also needed money to fight wars with other European powers. The colonists were not interested in paying for English ventures without being able to debate it first.

AN OLD WORLD WAR FOUGHT ACROSS THE WHOLE WORLD

The New World was carved up by the colonial powers into separate spheres of influence. The Spanish, French, and British were the main European powers throughout the Age of Colonialism who maintained settlements on the North American continent. Old World issues flared up, especially between France and Britain, which both had global territorial claims. In what is considered the first world war, Britain and France led competing coalitions (made up of the major European powers except for the Ottoman Empire), and the fighting, due to the vast empires of the competing nations, spanned five continents. Termed the Seven Years' War for its main fighting period lasting seven years (1756-1763) is known in the United States as the French and Indian War.

The North American theater's portion of the war may be identified by using the term French and Indian War, which saw the British colonial forces fighting against France and their Native allies. The French and British made conflicting claims on the land, even though the actual border was mostly undefined. The French offered to protect the Natives from further British incursions, and hence starting building forts. One such fort, named Fort Duquesne, was built at the meeting point of the Allegheny and Monongahela Rivers, that intersected to form the Ohio River. The area lies in the modern city of Pittsburgh, within the bounds of Pennsylvania. Pennsylvania was a British colony, and the building of a foreign military installation was met with resistance.

Virginia sent a militia to drive the French out. George Washington was the leader of the group, and they attacked a small French regimen, killing 10, including the commander. The French retaliated and forced Washington to surrender. The British and French (once the news reached Europe) tried to negotiated peace, but the negotiations failed. Both sides sent regular troops to North America to protect their claims. Meanwhile, the British were capturing French ships. The French intended to attack Hanover (in modern Germany) since the prince elector was also the British King. Prussia agreed to protect the city, and France, in a reversal of historical animosity, allied with Austria. As with all history, everything is connected and the rivalry between Prussia and Austria, which eventually led to a unified Germany excluding Austria in 1871, had already formed more than a century prior.

The British defeated the French in every campaign against New France. The group of Natives who had sided with the French resigned from the war in 1760 and negotiated a treaty to keep their trade routes between Canada and New York. The British eventually fully defeated the French forces and controlled the entire Eastern half of North America.

Chapter 4 – George Washington – The First President

After the Seven Years' War which saw the British successfully driving away the French from the English colonies in North America, the Crown found itself under a massive amount of debt. This prompted the British government to impose hefty taxes on their colonies so they can recoup their losses and somehow chip away at their national debt. The early Americans did not like these new taxes in the least; they cited that there should be "no taxation without representation in Parliament." However, the British government still pushed through with their plans, which understandably led to civil unrest. Things really got out of hand when some really ticked off Bostonians started throwing crates of tea into the Boston Harbor and effectively kicked off the Revolutionary War (an event that has had symbolic consequences to this day in the form of the conservatively political Tea Party in the United States).

The fledgling revolutionary army needed someone to lead them, someone who has enough guts to go against the British, and charismatic enough to inspire others to join their plight. The man they chose to become the general of the Continental army was none other than George Washington.

The Continental Congress, a convention of the delegates from the thirteen British colonies in North America, chose George Washington for the position of Commander in Chief of the Continental Army. Although he was born a British citizen, and he was a former redcoat, Washington's extreme dismay over the way the English are treating the colonists made him accept the post of Commander in Chief.

Before being offered the command position of the Continental Army, George Washington was a decorated British military veteran. In fact, he actually commanded troops of soldiers during the French and Indian War in 1754. Ironically,

Washington got help from the same people he engaged in battles before. He had already established himself as a worthy leader and strategic commander in a number of previous campaigns and it was because of his charismatic and seemingly stolid principles that he attracted respect from all sides, even though at heart he was not precisely a soldier. He had attempted a number of times to reenlist with the British Army but was turned down. Undeterred by this rejection, he instead devoted himself full heartedly to understanding and comprehending British military tactics, skills that would be invaluable to him later on when he would eventually turn the tides in the 1175 Revolution. In the years between the wars though he resorted to a simple and aristocratic life, marrying and having two children, and engaging in the leisurely activities of a gentlemen of the era which included, among other things, fox hunting.

Events would eventually draw him back into the political spheres of the Americas however, and in 1776 he began to voice concerns over the British sovereignty. This had included previous complains such as the effects of the Act Stamp of 1756 which imposed heavy taxes and whose constituents and delegations were made of primarily British citizens and no one from the colonies. Tensions were very palpable during these years, with many colonials apprehending that British involvement had become a sort of invasive presence in their lives. They still acted as though they owned the colonies, and both social and economic policies often put the colonists at a disadvantage. All of this was the perfect atmosphere for insurgence to flourish. The battles of Lexington and Concord actually marked the beginning of the war that would reshape the Americas forever and give birth to the new United States.

On June 14th, 1775 the Congress officially created the Continental Army and elected Washington as the Supreme Commander, in no small part because of his experience, but also because he had demonstrated and unprecedented loyalty and patriotism. Despite not having proper military training, and often under-supplied, Washington, through sheer force of will, managed to lead the Continental Army through a number of key victories. While there were true soldiers in his congregation, Washington did his best to recruit from the countryside as well, and it was actually the Prussian Commander from one of his previous campaigns that assumed the role of training them. Six years after he officially took the reins as commander-in-chief, the ragtag group of colonial rebels made the British forces surrender and allow the colonies to declare their independence.

There were a number of losses, but despite it all Washington never once retreated or surrendered, and his sense of pride in his generals and soldiers was legendary. One of these defeats happened to be at New York and resulted in huge losses for the Continental Army. The final and eventual peace came in 1784 when Britain signed the Treaty of Paris, a document that would grant the United States its independence from British rule and establish it as its own country. For Washington, the war was over. Thinking that he would return to his quiet life, history had other plans for him. In 1789 he was called out of his retirement by the Electoral College and officially elected as the first president of the United States.

One interesting feature was that they initially offered to pay him a salary that was equal to around $350,000 nowadays. Washington, although suffering financial troubles from his failing farm and homestead, actually rejected the offer at first, however he soon accepted it again – not so much because he needed the money but because he did not want to set a precedent for limiting the presidency only to those who were already wealthy enough, and requested that people only call him Mr. President (the most humble of the possible titles that had been conjured up by the Electoral College).

Before he retired as president however, Washington crafted one of the more endearing and famous documents, his Farewell Address. It listed out, among other things, his hopes for the United States (he was an avid advocate of republicanism, and actually feared the creation of a multi-party system of government, which he thought might weaken the union) and the importance law and the Constitution. One of the most lingering and influential aspects was probably his take on foreign policy, in which he took an insulator stance, thinking that it was not the place of Americans to interfere or get involved with the issues of other countries, and that they should only focus on American interest and activities.

Fun fact:

Although quite a number of history books mentions this "fact," George Washington's teeth are not really made of wood. For one thing, wood teeth would not have been very durable. The truth is, Washington's dentures were made of hippopotamus ivory, sometimes the teeth of pigs and monkeys were used, and they were set in lead. Washington's dentures were also said to be so uncomfortable that he had to resort to applying an opium-based liniment on his cheeks so he could bear the pain.

Chapter 5 – The Founding Fathers and the Signing of the Declaration of Independence

In the summer of 1776, delegates from each of the original thirteen colonies, also known as the Second Continental congress, gathered in Philadelphia. The goal of the group is to decide whether it is the right time for the colonies to secede from England. The past year was an incredibly hard one for the young United States, as they have been constantly battling the much better equipped and trained British redcoats, but somehow the tides turned in their favor, and they forced the colonizers to retreat.

Richard Henry Lee, the delegate from Virginia, proposed a resolution of independence. The Lee resolution is the earliest known draft of what would be the Declaration of Independence. The resolution stated that the United Colonies are no longer under the rule of the British and that any and all allegiances with the British Crown were immediately dissolved.

The Committee of Five

During the drafting period of the Declaration, not all of the delegates had the authority to vote on what goes into the document, as their states haven't given them the power to do so. While they were still figuring things out, the Continental Congress appointed a committee consisting of the five most brilliant minds in the nation; Benjamin Franklin, Thomas Jefferson, John Adams, Roger Sherman, and Robert Livingston.

At first, the delegates wanted Richard Henry Lee to draft the Declaration of Independence. However, certain events happened that prevented Lee from penning what would have been the single most important document in American history. Fortunately, a young delegate from Virginia by the name of

Thomas Jefferson was up to the task. Initially, Jefferson wanted John Adams to write the declaration, but when the latter refused, Jefferson forced himself to do the task.

Because this was taking place in the wake of a newly found independence, it was a period of liminal political movements. Basically, there were still many citizens who, though professing their love for their independence, still held shaky and tenuous allegiances and loyalties to the king. The Declaration of Independence in its form included a number of paragraphs and entries that attempted to further separate the United States from its British founder, and this happened to be a `right to revolution`. While a number of colonists hoped that they would eventually be able to reconcile with Europe and the British monarchy, it was clear to the patriots and the Committee of Five that this was an opportunity to once and for all truly grasp their liberation.

The Committee of Five worked tirelessly for almost a month until, on June 28, 1776, they published the final draft of the Declaration of Independence and presented it to Congress. What is interesting to note, and testament to the integrity of the founding fathers, was that the document actually contained no new information or ideas; it consisted primarily in its final draft of ideas and thoughts and principles that had all been widely exercised and held dear during the American Revolution – one of the primary being a sense of oppression from Britain, and especially King George who was seen as having undermined the God-given rights of the colonists.

Some of the later effects of the Declaration of Independence would surface in the form of a controversial take on slavery. One of the most famous passages, that "all men are born equal" has often been taken to insist that Jefferson was condemning the British act of slavery, and in fact a number of paragraphs that further admonished Britain for it were eventually deleted from the final document – while this has historically been proven accurate, the real irony is that Jefferson himself was a prominent slave owner with hundreds of indentured slaves under his control. Whatever the intent, the Declaration of Independence would eventually serve as a banner for future abolitionists, one of the most famous and iconic being, of course, Abraham Lincoln.

Fun facts:

The Continental Congress officially adopted the Declaration of Independence on the Fourth of July in 1776, but the Founding Fathers did not get a chance to sign it until a good part of a month has passed by. Additionally, one of the signers John Hancock, whose very elegant signature appeared on the document, became embedded in the cultural milieu of the United States and today the word 'Hancock' is synonymous with someone's signature.

Here's another lesser known fact: one signer of the Declaration, Richard Stockton, recanted his signature on the document and withdrew his support from the Revolution. However, he did it not because he wanted to. On November 30, 1776, just months after the signing of the Declaration, British troops captured Stockton and threw him in prison. His captors "convinced" Stockton to rescind from the Revolution by limiting his food rations and torturing him until he swore his allegiance to King George III.

Chapter 6 – A Half Century of Expansion: 1803-1853

Following the American Revolution, the colonies became their own power. The territorial expanse of the newly-formed nation was greater than any of the old powers proper in Europe except Russia. However, the United States had a lot of growing to do before it became the continent-spanning nation that it is today. Between the American Revolution and the American Civil War, the United States expanded its area from the East Coast colonies all the way across the continent to California, coming into conflict with the claims still laid by the old European powers.

LOUISIANA PURCHASE

Not long after the Revolutionary War, the United States was presented the opportunity to purchase a huge swath of land that stretched from Montana to Louisiana from the French. The purchase effectively doubled the land area of the United States and gave the new country a wealth of natural resources.

Jefferson wanted control of New Orleans, a French city, because it was at the mouth of the Mississippi River. This would give American farmers from inland a better route to transport goods either to Europe or to the East Coast, where the majority of the population lived. Jefferson's first offer to purchase the city was rejected, but when he made another offer, this one five-fold the original, it was accepted. France even offered to sell the rest of the territory for just a 50% premium. France sold New Orleans for $10 million and the other 828,000 square miles of the territory for another $5 million.

Napoleon needed the money for his wars and to, of course, fight Britain. The French had also recently regained control of the area from Spain, which they had ceded as a result of the Seven Years' War. This reestablished control was worrying to the nascent United States because France was now resurgent under Napoleon and American farmers in the Ohio River Valley relied on access to the Mississippi River and New Orleans. However, Napoleon was willing to give up the territory which cost France a significant amount to maintain for the equivalent of $15 billion. This marked the end of any sort of French colonial power in the United States, and is widely regarded as one of the most extreme geopolitical blunders in modern history.

TEXAS ANNEXATION AND MEXICAN AND SPANISH CESSIONS

The United States was at this point far larger than any of its European counterparts, again except Russia. The nation was not done growing, yet, though. Spain still held territory in Florida, but their strength in the Americas was weakening, and the Spanish were not interested in investing further in the colony.

This led to the cession of Florida from Spain, again in a diplomatic way instead of war. Surely military conflict was not absent, as tribes and escaped slaves had been raiding Georgia (originally created as a buffer to the lucrative Carolinas), and American troops had made incursions into the Spanish territory. Spain was unable to control the area and hence it was more susceptible to relinquishing control of the land. A few American politicians demanded Spain give up Texas, too, but that would have to wait 26 years.

The cession of Florida was not a purchase, like Louisiana, but the United States agreed to pay legal claims from American citizens gain Spain up to $5 million and gave Spanish goods preferential tariff treatment at Floridian ports. Under the treaty, named the Adams-Onís Treaty, Spain was granted secured control over Texas west to California. The area had originally been a point of dispute between Spain and the United States, as the United States claimed the Louisiana Purchase had granted control to the Rocky Mountains.

Under Manifest Destiny and the march towards the 42nd Parallel (of latitude), the United States lost some territory to Britain in the area north of modern Montana. This now lies within Canada, which, at the time of the cession, was still part of Britain.

Shortly before the American Civil War, Texas was annexed by the United States. The state was a large slave-holding independent Republic, which had declared itself separate from Mexico in 1836. The political climate of the United States at the time was tumultuous, with the divide between the industrial North and agricultural South already having been developed. The addition of Texas would significantly add to the southern side's power, and it was opposed by Northern politicians. Nonetheless, Texas became part of American territory in 1845, much to the celebration of most Texans, who favored entry into the Union. The Texans were largely Americans who had moved into Mexican territory on the invitation of the Mexican government, who wanted to populate the area.

Not long after the Texas Annexation, Britain ceded the Oregon territories to the United States (1846) in another Manifest Destiny treaty. Two years later, Mexico gave up its claim to the American Southwest after a very long and bloody war, which mostly rounded out the current shape of the Lower 48. The area along the Rio Grande, still part of Mexican territory, was purchased by the United States in 1853 in order to complete a transcontinental railway. The last two additions, Hawaii and Alaska, would have to wait until after the American Civil War.

One of the primary reasons for this massive expansion, and its invariable success, had a lot to do with the American sense of a new freedom and independence. Suddenly the entire country was theirs, and with so much of the territory owned or operated by foreign powers, the obvious conclusion was it would be easier to simply purchase it themselves. It was often a costly process to run colonies, and unless they were centrally located and able to supply a very high-in-demand product (such as tea in India), the risk-loss ratios were rarely worth it – especially now in the pre-Industrial era when new technologies were being developed – and for many foreign colonial powers it might have come as an actual relief to not have to worry about these distant outposts.

Also contributing to this massive expansion was the fact that America had proved its worth in the American Revolution against, then, one of the most powerful global powers in the world: Britain. Many of the outlying colonial powers, like France, were as we've seen already engaged in other battles and wars elsewhere, and the idea of going to war with the patriotic willpower of the Americans was not attractive. Lastly, for the colonists themselves, a sense of Manifest Destiny had given them a newfound sense of purpose; numerous towns spread west, and in the more remote areas where it was difficult to maintain supply lines, it had suddenly become necessary to invest in their new country (in terms of transportation, etc.).

Chapter 7 – The Trail of Tears

In 1830, then President Andrew Jackson signed into law the Indian Removal Act of 1830. This law permitted the evacuation and relocation (often forceful) of the Native American people from their native lands into a single large settlement in Oklahoma. There were two reasons why Jackson signed this infamous bill. One was so the government could sell the lands formerly owned by the Native Americans to the settlers, mainly because there were reports of gold in the area.

The other reason was the recommendation of the former President James Monroe. In his last speech to Congress, Monroe emphasized the need to relocate the Native American people because he feels they are stopping the migration of settlers westward, and it seemed like Jackson believed the same thing.

Upon its passing, the Indian Removal Act effectively kicked out almost 125,000 Native Americans, mostly from the Cherokee nation, from their ancestral homes in Georgia, and sent the people, both young and old, trekking thousands of miles on foot towards their new settlements in Oklahoma. An estimated 4,000 Native Americans died, either through exhaustion, hunger, or exposure, while on the way to Oklahoma. This huge number of casualties is what led to this forced exodus to get the moniker "The Trail of Tears."

What effect did the Trail of Tears have on the Native American people?

Besides the forced relocation, the Native Americans were also forced to adapt to the dynamics of a new economic system that is completely alien to their original beliefs. For instance, the Native Americans must come to terms that land can be bought and sold, it is no longer something that one must hold onto and protect for future generations of his family. The different conceptual ideas and whole cosmogony of the natives differed from the Manifest Destiny philosophy of the newly independent United States.

For many Native Americans, the land was not something to own but rather something to be respected, and they thought of their relationship to it as symbiotic. By displacing a people, they were actually destroying the *culture*, something so valuable that once it was lost or destroyed there was very little way to get it back.

Were there tribes that opposed the Indian Removal Act?

Of course, numerous Native Americans were averse to the new law that forced them to leave their homes, one of which was the Cherokee tribe. The Cherokees tried to fight the Indian Removal Act. They filed a case against the entire state of Georgia, and it eventually found its way to the Supreme Court where Justice John Marshall declared that the government had no right to claim the Cherokee's ancestral lands as its own. Unfortunately, President Jackson overruled this declaration and allowed it to push through.

A number of other nations also rose up, including the Seminole people who had lived in the Florida area. A militia of 500 men were organized to deal with the 'Indian problem', but the Seminoles were a hardy and fierce people, and their guerilla tactics ended up working initially. They would capture supply lines and burn plantations, which actually helped to boost their numbers as freed slaves would then join their cause. The decade of fighting would be a bloody and gruesome affair for both sides, with the United States government and army dedicating nearly $20,000,000 to the fight – this number was almost unheard of, and in today's market would be equivalent to nearly $491,000,000. And while the Seminole Indian bands did suffer great casualties, they do represent a certain victory in the native history of the United States since the government and army eventually gave up fighting them. To this day, they still proudly consider themselves the only native peoples in North America to have never relinquished their sovereignty or signed a peace treaty.

One of the major problems with these treaties was first that often the leaders of the tribes did not speak for all of their members, and second many of the chiefs were manipulated or coerced into signing the treaties that may or may not have represented their best interests. There are also countless instances in American history involving certain conditionals – for example, a number of nations in what is now Oregon were given a choice between signing a treaty that said they gave up their ancestral lands and had to move, or going to war with the local military station there. Additionally, many treaties were found to be 'signed' by the chiefs, who only later realized that the magistrates in control had forged their signatures entirely. The original treaties that took place on the east coast would set a precedent for nearly two hundred years involving the slow and gradual attrition of native land.

The Trail of Tears is the worst case of human rights violations to happen to the Native American population. Not only were they forced to leave the lands they used to call their home, but they were also given little to no compensation in exchange of their relocation.

Chapter 8 – Abraham Lincoln, the Emancipation Proclamation, and the American Civil War

According to the Declaration of Independence, "... all men are created with and equal right to liberty". However, President Abraham Lincoln had his doubts if whether the people really understood what that part of the declaration meant, because as of that time, the United States was the largest country in the world where it was still legal to own slaves, although in the North it had been banned since 1803. The political landscape at the time was a tumultuous one because there was a great division between how to approach slavery, with the South very much in favor it. In his famous Peoria Speech delivered on October 16th, 1854 Lincoln (who had previously disagreed with his nemesis Stephen A. Douglas on letting each state legislate its own laws about slavery, as opposed to having Congress dictate the matter) finally spoke out and made his stance clear. This would come back later in his famous Douglas-Lincoln debates in 1858 in which Lincoln attempted to decry the act of slavery as being something that undermined the principals not only of republicanism but of the founding fathers real message about 'all mean being created equally'.

Although a somewhat awkward looking president (he was extremely tall to the average person), Lincoln quickly proved himself not only a capable intellectual but also a skilled orator, and is considered even today to be among one of the best speakers that the United States has ever produced. His campaign for presidency was fraught with problems, but at last on November 6, 1860 he was elected the 16th President. That following December a number of the secession states in the South who had opposed his nomination declared themselves a separate confederacy, which was technically illegal. Attempts were made to reconcile, but it was clear that the country was "sitting on a volcano".

The American Civil War, which was probably the bloodiest war to ever happen in the United States, started because the free and slave-owning states could not reach an agreement. Abraham Lincoln, a Republican whose platform was to abolish slavery throughout the entire country, had won the presidency but the country was divided. Understandably, President Lincoln and the states from the Northern territories refused to recognize the Confederacy and questioned its legitimacy. They feared that this secession would strike a negative blow to the image of democracy and that it would result in the "United" States to split into several smaller countries that would constantly be at each other's throats.

The actual Civil War started when the Confederates attacked Fort Sumter in Charleston Bay and forced them to lower the American flag. Lincoln did not take too kindly at this act of aggression, so he called out the militia to suppress the insurgents. After this encounter, four more slave states seceded from the Union and joined the Confederacy. That stage was set for war.

Things got really messy starting on 1862. Huge battles like the ones that happened in Shiloh, Tennessee, Gaines' Mill, and Fredericksburg Virginia resulted in heavy casualties on both sides. By 1864, the Union Army's original goal of a limited battle to restore the United States changed to an all-out war to destroy the Old South and its tradition of slavery.

During the onset of the Civil War, both sides seemed to have an equal chance of winning, but after three long years, the Confederacy started losing steam. When General Ulysses S. Grant became the commanding general of the entire Union army, things began to shift in their favor. Lincoln had set up a number of blockades which had effectively cut off the supply lines and support to the South. General Grant's relentless attacks on the South's great General Robert E. Lee proved too much for the latter to handle.

[35]

By springtime of 1865, the Confederate armies started to surrender one-by-one. On May 10, 1865, the Union army cornered and captured the fleeing president of the Confederacy, Jefferson Davis. With Davis's capture, all the remaining resistance fighters dropped their weapons and surrendered. Finally, after years of war, and hundreds of thousands of American soldiers killed, the United States could finally start the painful process of rebuilding the nation.

LINCOLN'S EMANCIPATION PROCLAMATION

When Robert E. Lee's forces eventually managed to cross the Potomac River in 1862 something shifted in the struggle. The eventual victory by the Union over Lee's forces at this battle was one of the bloodiest in the entire war, but it was a resounding boost in Lincoln's favor. This was the perfect excuse and opportunity for Lincoln to put into play the ace up his sleeve. On July 22, 1862, Abraham Lincoln, dressed in his trademark dark frock coat, convened the members of his cabinet and confided to them that he had "dwelt much and long" on the subject of owning slaves in the United States of America. Then, Lincoln, speaking in measured tones, read the first draft of what would become known as The Emancipation Proclamation, the piece of legislation that effectively made it illegal to own slaves in the United States. He had actually drafted and written the document quite a while before, but for a number of strategic reasons he had never broached it or put it forward, fearing that to do so while in the middle of a war – and especially in the wake of a possible loss – might constitute a sign of desperation to his supporters.

On September 22, 1862, Lincoln issued a preliminary proclamation that was essentially a warning to the states which would not end their rebellion. He said that after a hundred days has passed and they would not cease their secession, Lincoln would order the emancipation of all the slaves in their respective states. The Emancipation

Proclamation obviously outraged the white Southerners who owned slaves, it angered some Northern democrats, undermined the efforts of European forces to supply aid to the Confederacy, and it lifted the spirits of millions of African-Americans, both slaves and free men. Around 1862 mid-term elections were also, however, underway, and while the Republicans themselves were a bit disgruntled by the way things were going, Democrats saw it as an opportunity to weaken Lincoln. Already the Republicans had managed to infuriate a number of states with high taxes, inflation, and with a martial law that acted to conscript citizens into the Union Army.

Nevertheless, with a continual winning streak over the Confederacy Lincoln's Emancipation Proclamation became a military goal, and would result in almost 3 million slaves being freed. Lincoln even had the dream of developing colonies especially for freed slaves, although this was never realized. Still, it is important to note that a number of freed slaves eventually joined the ranks of the Union Army. At one point one of Lincoln's generals took it upon himself to create 20 regiments of black soldiers, and they would end up playing a pivotal role in bringing the war to its eventual conclusion.

GETTYSBURG ADDRESS

Following another victory in Gettysburg, Lincoln appeared before hundreds of citizens and delivered another enthralling speech that would go down in history as one of the most poignant and self-affirming of American beliefs. It asserted things that he had already talked about and strove to embody, but more than anything it also offered some hope, as he now envisioned the Civil War as not only being about ending slavery, but also heralding the 'new birth of freedom in the nation'.

THE END OF THE WAR AND THE 13TH AMENDMENT

In a war of attrition, the end finally came about reluctantly. Still focused on expelling and defeating the Confederacy, Lincoln was almost single-minded in his resolution. And yet, at the same time, his approach to how to deal with newly captured Confederacy territory was both wise and compassionate, and was quoted in answer to how they should treat the defeated shoulders as saying "Let 'em up easy". This went hand in hand with his desire for true unification of the United States, and he understood that all the states would have to work together; at the same time he sent commanders to these captured states to ensure that both moderate and radicals alike would not cause any more trouble.

At last, the war had ended. In achieving this victory, Lincoln's greatest achievement was in introducing the banning of slavery into effective law for the *entire* United States. Although the first attempt to pass a law banning all slavery did not go through, the second time Congress finally agreed, and December 6, 1856 it was ratified and became the 13th Amendment to the American Constitution.

LINCOLN'S DEATH AND HIS LEGACY

Perhaps the only thing more famous than what Lincoln was able to accomplish in his time as president was how he eventually died. While attending the theater on April 14th, 1865, he was assassinated by John Wilkes Booth, five days after the complete surrender of Robert E. Lee and his Confederate Armies. Booths took the opportunity when the president was alone in his booth and shot him point blank, killing him instantly. Later Booth was tracked down and shot when he refused to surrender. Nevertheless, Lincoln's career and his pivotal role in helping to shape the economic, political, and social atmosphere of the United States lived on, and was both an icon and martyr to future abolitionists and human rights activists.

Fun fact:

Although most history books do not mention them, there were Native Americans that fought on both sides of the Civil War. In fact, quite a number of them held high positions in the army. For instance, Stand Watie was a Cherokee Indian who was promoted to the rank of brigadier general in the Confederate Army, and he was actually the last Confederate general to surrender.

Another interesting fact is that one of the primary Cherokee leaders, a man named Tsali, gained a reputation among the Americans and his own people for not only encouraging the Cherokee to side with other nations in their struggle, but also for being a prophet. During the Indian Removal Act, a number of soldiers came to the homesteads owned by his family, and several of them were attacked and killed. As a result, Tsali was condemned for his part in the insurrection by other Cherokee bands and eventually hunted down and executed.

Chapter 9 – Reconstruction and the Gilded Age

NORTH AND SOUTH STILL DIVIDED

The Civil War was not kind to the southern States. The infamous Sherman's March devastated a large swath of the south, and the emancipation of the slave populations did not bode well for the economy of the regions, as they were heavily dependent on slave labor to produce such huge yields of cash crops. No longer having an indentured population of workers, many plantations fell into disuse and disrepair and were unable to keep their quotas. Many former slaves did not have a much better life free, as they were released to live on a small tract of land owned by former owners and required to pay a sort of tax on their crop yields to said owners. Rather than a brand new life of independence and freedom, these ex-slaves found themselves chained to a different sort of shackle, that of economic dependence on their old masters and an inflexibility in terms of economic mobility (in other words, they were often drained of any excess cash, and only made just enough money to get by, meaning they would never be able to advance in the world).

Immediately following the Civil War, the effort to rebuild the South was underway (it is not advantageous to a country for half of it to lay in ruins). The South pushed through many political reforms known as "black codes," which even required former slaves to sign yearly labor contracts or face arrest. In Mississippi, a contract had to be signed for the following year, and if the contracted left before the end of the year, earlier wages would be forfeit. In South Carolina, the only contracts open to former slaves were for farm labor or servants, unless they paid a tax of $10 to $100. Of course, this was the 1860s, and these were former slaves who had absolutely no assets to their names. Moreover, for employers, there were various versions of "anti-enticement," which sought to punish those who offered higher wages for employees on contracts of others.

The victorious North were furious over the laws which kept many African Americans oppressed and only nominally out of slavery. The anger led to Radical Reconstruction, which saw Northern ideals forced on the South. From 1867 Congress took over reconstruction from the executive branch and started to implement more free-labor ideals. The more liberal policies led to a backlash in the South, one result being the formation of the infamous Ku Klux Klan. For whites, especially those that had had prominent holdings in slave labor, it was like their new government was suddenly disenfranchising them, a cruel twist of irony considering this was the same thing they had been exercising on their slaves for the past century. As abolitionist sentiment began to overtake the United States, especially in the north, this only helped widen the gap between whites and blacks in the south, often leading to violent confrontations and very strong racism.

INDUSTRIALIZATION AND NEW WAGE SLAVES

The United States was not to be left behind from its European brethren. The huge land area and resources offered by the country bode well for its industrial base. The large differential between wages in Europe and America enticed millions of Europeans to emigrate to the United States in the late 19th century. These immigrants filled the jobs the new American industrial engine offered. During this period of progress, huge advances in industrialization and mechanization were underway, especially in terms of agriculture. Unlike the crowded countries of the Europe, North America and the United States offered an unprecedented opportunity for expansion, and spurred on by their relationship with the rest of the world it really was a 'cash crop' economy. It was also abundantly easy for random ordinary folk to try their hand at farming, and before long the Mid-west was a thriving

[41]

agricultural center focusing on any number of crops. It wouldn't be long before many farmers realized that it was more profitable to focus on a single crop, and this was evidence of a new type of a specialization. With the advent of technological marvels that could help farms and increase the efficiency of farms, it also made it possible produce a lot more surplus and helped ease the lives of workers.

Railroads allowed the cross continental industry to arise, with the western lands producing minerals and other raw materials for the factories in the old North. It is hard to overstate the effects that steam and coal power had on shaping the new frontiers. Those distant homesteads and towns, especially out toward the West, could now be accessed much easier. In order to help this, the government invested heavily in producing more and more railroads. Often times it would take the form of land grants which were given to companies. In exchange this let them build through federal lend and increased the overall wealth of the population.

 The South continued to suffer the aftereffects of the Civil War, and while wages rose for immigrants filling jobs in factories, the former slaves in the South were left disadvantaged. These millions of immigrants and many millions of Americans flooded into cities, where the work was located. The notorious tenements of major cities arose, and the American industrial base started to overtake those in Europe. With the railroads and vast natural resources, America moved into heavy industry, and the steel production of America raced ahead to become more significant than the outputs of Britain, France, and Germany combined. The old colonial powers Britain and France invested heavily in the railroads, which further expanded American industrial dominance.

However, it was not just steel and coal that moved on those trains. Crops from the central United States and livestock were ferried across vast distances to be processed in the newly built cities. Additionally, it was also a great transportation hub for moving soldiers and militia, as well as building equipment to border towns. During the hey-day of the railroad boom it was also even used in conjunction with the American Postal Service as a way to get mail across the country. As more money was needed to build and invest, finance became ever more important in the new American economy. The fledgling nation that had just a mere 100 years earlier been a small competitor to the Great Powers in Europe was now charging ahead to take center stage on numerous global affairs, both economic and technological. The new immigrants to the United States, as well as those already living there, pumped out a continuous, voluminous flow of new inventions to shape the new era of modernization.

The term Gilded Age comes from the notion that not all was well in the new era. Indeed, prosperity skyrocketed, but wealth inequality led to numerous conflicts. The Labor Movement fought for better working conditions and an end to abusive labor practices. The Robber Barons, businessmen who amassed great wealth on the backs of workers, permeated the era. While they helped catapult America to the forefront of all things economic, the human cost was heavy. The name itself derives from the thief (robber) and a type of nobility (baron), which should not be present in a political system based on democracy. These men built huge empires and wealth for themselves while giving very little to their workers. Some became philanthropists who donated a significant portion back to the communities in the form of institutions that still stand today.

The new industrial might of the United States would serve it well during the 20th century when it produced huge armaments and further built out the industry that helped the United States become a superpower.

Chapter 10 – Constant Wars and Security

In 1898 the United States fought a war with Spain, which was completely unprepared for the conflict in its distant colonies. Cuba had wanted to split from Spain and the United States declared its right to do so. Shortly thereafter, the war erupted, and the United States defeated Spain. Cuba gained independence from Spain and was left outside American territory. The United States was not only concerned with Cuba, though.

Guam and Puerto Rico were lost to the United States, which are still under some form of American control. The much more populous Philippines were purchased by the United States for $20 million, and suddenly America had far-flung assets around the globe. The United States had become a global player and less than 120 years after its own independence, the nation had risen to prominence to rival Europe. The relative insulation from European wars and the vast expanse of resources and land afforded the United States, along with its freedoms and wages that enticed large numbers of skilled labor, such a position. While the Monroe Doctrine in 1823 warned European powers to stay out of Western Hemisphere politics, the United States could now force Europe to stay out of such affairs. Furthermore, the United States could dictate terms across the globe.

WORLD WAR I

The United States, surrounded by two vast oceans, kept itself mostly out of European politics. When World War I broke out between the various powers in Europe, the United States remained staunchly neutral. The American public had little interest in fighting a war that was not their own, and life in America was, in general, good. The centuries-old rivalries between European powers were not meant to be solved by American troops. At this time the United States was still reeling from its own American Civil War and there was little reason politically or economically to enter the theater of another conflict.

However, as the war in Europe raged on it became clear that there were a number of things at stake, and America became more and more politically interested. Under Kaiser Wilhelm, the German Empire, itself recently formed, wanted to build itself into a global power just as the United States had and its neighbors had had for a long time. This inevitably meant conflict Germany and Britain and France. The United States wanted to stay neutral, but Britain was a close trading partner and Germany had blockaded the Isles in an attempt to defeat Britain. This was especially pertinent to the burgeoning industries of the United States, and in particular agriculture – many of the farmers and new agricultural steads of land and companies relied heavily on foreign export in order to remain prosperous. Germany had officially cut off this resource, and in order to enforce the blockade started to attack any ship, neutral or hostile, on the high seas. The military power of Britain lay in its navy, and Germany needed to defeat this.

Unfortunately, this included passenger ships carrying Americans. Following two torpedo attacks against ships carrying American passengers including the infamous and ill-fated *Lusitania*, public opinion in America turned against Germany and there was a social and political movement that supported joining the other nations against Germany. Before this there had been a sharp division in terms of citizens, many of them thinking it would be unwise to partake in a war so far overseas. In the previous War of 1812, America had seen firsthand how costly and expensive it was to wage a conflict that was not in easy proximity to one's forces. However, following a resumption of German hostilities against non-combative ships, the United States eventually entered World War I on the side of the Allies. The irony however was that America at this time was not a particularly strong military presence – aside from the casualties incurred by the American

Civil War, the US had also been threatening Mexico and its army and navy were quite small in comparison to a super power like Britain. Nevertheless, overcoming political barriers, Woodrow Wilson eventually managed to pass a national declaration of war which passed on April 6th, 1917. What was interesting about their move however was that, even though they fought with other allied nations, the US remained staunchly independent in regards to its own diplomacy.

By this time the Allies were weary after having fought for so long, so the arrival of American troops was a godsend, sometimes arriving in fleets of as many 10,000 troops a day. Because WWI had been fought as a sort of 'attrition' conflict through the use of trench warfare, many of the Allied troop movements had slowed or incurred such devastating losses that for all parties involved an end to hostilities was the primary goal. Coming to the war three years and millions of dead Europeans late, the United States, with its huge, untouched-by-war industrial base and population, burst onto the European scene and helped end the war within a little over a year. The final attack came in the Hundred Days Offensive and would mark the end of the German offensive until WWI a decade and a half later.

LEAGUE OF NATIONS AND AN ERA OF PROSPERITY

The introduction of mechanized warfare and the seemingly purposeless deaths of millions drove the desire to end the war. World War I was termed the Great War and the War to End All Wars, because it was hoped this display of brutal, efficient, mechanized death would once and forever stop the march of bloody conflict.

One attempt to end the war between nations was to create a place for them to practice diplomacy before resorting to war. While the United States, for the most part, was uninjured in the war and wanted to implement a lasting and just peace, Britain and France wanted revenge for the deaths of millions of their citizens and the destruction of their lands by German ambition. The US President, Woodrow Wilson, wanted the United States to lead the League of Nations, but, due to legal demands deemed unconstitutional by Congress, the League was created without the United States. As a result, Woodrow simply signed independent peace treaties with the other countries involved.

The exclusion of the United States from the League was by no means a problem for the United States. During the 1920s, as Europe was still recovering from the war, American culture and economy flourished. The wealth of the United States doubled within a decade, and a great many Americans were granted access to a consumer culture. The country was now more than half an urban population and people across the entire continent formed an American culture thanks to nationwide advertising and the communication links provided by new technology. Many were averse to the mass culture that was enveloping the nation, but the idea of consumerism had taken hold.

There was conflict; one of the most famous being Prohibition. Responding to a wave of temperance movements, various states had already enacted their own forms of restriction on alcohol. A lot of the impetus came from a Protestant atmosphere that saw alcohol as being the root of evil and excess, and in the 1920's a prohibition was signed into law, becoming the 18th Amendment to the American Constitution, banning and forbidding the manufacture, sale, or transportation of alcoholic liquids and several states had strict laws regarding even possession of alcoholic substances. The ban led to a loss of tax revenue and various criminal activities, as people were heartily attached to alcohol. At the same time, it seemed like a good idea to many: the previous 19th century domestic scene had been marked by alcoholism, family violence, and 'saloon style' corruption in politics. This created a divide in post-WWI America between the drys and the wets, or those who advocated Prohibition and those who didn't.

The main problem was that Prohibition targeted the lower class much more than the middle or wealthy in society. A rich person could safely and easily keep or hide alcohol inside his house, but the penalties on possession for the poor was high and their access to it was diminished, causing public outrage. This led to the practice of 'bootlegging' which was the illegal creation, distribution, and selling of alcohol. Many people made their own and a whole black market economy developed, even going so far as to smuggle alcohol across the Canadian border. In some more blue-collar neighborhoods, it also led to the creation of 'speak easy' establishments, often run by ex-bar owners who would sell their products secretly to those who wanted a drink. One of the most famous players in the whole Prohibition racket was the eponymous Al Capone who, along with a number of others, basically ran Chicago and were actively involved in the boot-legging industry.

Eventually, even the main proponents of Prohibition realized it wasn't working. First of all, it was causing a lot of strife between classes. Secondly, there was really very little way to efficiently police the ban on alcohol. And lastly, and most importantly, it was a very reliable cash crop as well. Before Prohibition's inception, almost 14% of the GDP had been earned off of the production and selling of alcohol. As a result, Prohibition was eventually repealed, turning over the 18th amendment and bringing in the new 21st Amendment.

Chapter 11 – The Great Depression

The United States of America is now one of the strongest economies in the world today, but that wasn't always the case. There was a time when the economy of the US took such a huge hit that suicide statistics rose to an unprecedented number; that time was known as The Great Depression, the darkest ten years in US economy.

How it started

Even though the Great Depression happened decades ago, economists are still debating about its actual cause/s. The most common belief is that it all started right after the 1929 crash of the stock market, ominously remembered as Black Tuesday. During the roaring 20's, right after World War I, rural Americans started moving into the cities because of the sudden boom in the industrial sector. However, while the cities did become more prosperous, it also led to overproduction on the agricultural side. It was a time of excess, back then the people thought that the stock market would only continue to rise, this despite numerous speculations from financial experts. Other theorists point out that low income and employment coupled with a banking crisis in which nearly a third of banks effectively disappeared.

The problem was, in such a volatile economy, if one bank happened to go broke, it created a chain reaction, sort of like dominoes running into one another. Once this process picked up momentum, it would become impossible to stop, which is exactly what happened. Some economists including Milton Friedman suggested that the Federal Reserve was to blame for not bailing out banks by lending them money in order to stay afloat. One of the primary reasons that the Federal Reserve couldn't do this, however, was that in order to print new money they would be violating the 'gold standard' which said they needed to have a certain amount of backing – almost 40% - on notes that they produced and sent out.

Then things started to go south; the steel manufacturers' production slowed down, the construction sector was sluggish, the automobile industry wasn't selling as many units as they used to, and the people are racking up huge debts. Despite all of these bad omens, companies continued to sell their stocks, and the people continued buying them in the hopes of striking it rich.

On September 20, 1929, the London Stock Exchange crashed following the arrest and conviction of top British investors for fraud and forgery. This caused a panic in American investors because the huge volume of stocks sold at London caused the prices in the ticker tapes in America to be hours late. This widespread panic caused financial experts to advise the people to get out of the market; on October 29 of that same year, almost 16 million shares of stocks were traded, but some of them had no buyers at any price. The stock market lost more than $30 billion in just two days; it was the biggest stock market crash ever experienced in the USA.

After the crash

Several years after the Black Tuesday, people started feeling the effects. Consumer spending drastically declined, which caused industrial production to go down as well, and this resulted in the laying off of hundreds of thousands of workers. By 1933, the Great Depression was at its peak; almost 15 million Americans were unemployed, and almost half of the country's banking institutions have permanently closed shop. It was a very dark time in America. Hundreds of people would show up at bread lines and soup kitchens in the once wealthy cities. Ironically, farmers in the rural areas could not even afford to harvest their crops, which meant they had to let all that good food rot in their fields while millions of people were starving.

This also had a huge effect on the social makeup of the United States, in particular the role of women. Many of the major industries were primarily occupied by men, and since these were the first to go, it often fell to the women to pick up the slack. This took a number of forms: although there were some women in white-collar jobs who experienced less lay-offs, most tried to do their best to try and find a way to make enough money just to get by. In rural areas and even in bigger cities women would often do their best to grow their own vegetables and small gardens in order to supplement the cost of food. A whole culture of thriftiness, in sharp contrast to the luxurious spending spree culture of the 1920's, began to evolve. Learning how to get by with minimal resources, fixing clothes, re-using items, and re-purposing things that would normally be thrown away became the staple. Many married woman also joined the labor force in positions that were normally held by men – a trend that would continue, and become vital and indispensable, with the coming of the next world war. Most countries soon began to recover around 1933 and fortunately things started to change for the better when Franklin D. Roosevelt took his oath as the President of the United States.

A ray of hope

Immediately after taking his oath of office, Franklin Delano Roosevelt started working on healing the US economy. First, he announced a four-day "bank holiday" that forced all the banks to temporarily close so that Congress will have enough time to pass legislation that will help them recover. Furthermore, FDR created the Federal Deposit Insurance Corporation (FDIC) to provide security and protection for bank depositors and the Securities and Exchange Commission (SEC) to serve as a guard dog for the stock market and thus prevent similar abuses that led to the 1929 stock market crash that caused the Great Depression.

He is most famous, however, for his economic solution to the Great Depression which became known as the New Deal. These took the form primarily of new industrial projects and it was the first step in bringing the Federal Government into a more active economic role in the country. Many of the projects he spearheaded included new infrastructure, in particular the development of roads and bridges, but also specific construction projects. In fact, one fun fact is that the Timberline Lodge which is located on the south face of Mt. Hood was one of his ideas – he looked on the Great Depression as a terrible failure on behalf of the government to help its citizens, but also realized it was an opportunity to get the US back on track with building projects that would increase its economic growth and give people, most importantly, a sense of hope. The Timberline Lodge, in this case, was one such example. With the support of local workers, it would become a shining beacon of FDR's New Deal politics.

But there were a number of drastic actions taken as well. Probably the biggest and most controversial move that FDR made was taking the US economy off the gold standard, and making it illegal for ordinary citizens to own gold. Executive Order 6102 forbids the hoarding of gold, in any of its forms, in the continental United States. The reasoning for this EO was it would help remove the constraint preventing the Federal Reserve from increasing the supply of money in circulation.

Fun Fact: Executive Order 6102 is the reason why the 1933 gold double eagle coin is such a rarity today. Almost all of the known specimens of this rare coin were smelted back down into bars during the Great Depression so finding one now in good condition is almost like winning the jackpot in the lottery. In fact, one 1933 gold double eagle in excellent condition was sold at a 2002 Sotheby's auction for a whopping $7.6 million.

The unexpected benefit of World War II

When the United States eventually got dragged into World War II, the government started spending huge amounts of money in militarization. This sudden financial windfall rejuvenated the American steel industries and weapons manufacturers; after years of unemployment, US citizens finally had jobs. This claim is quite controversial as many historians disagree with the claim that WWII ended the Great Depression. Instead, they believe that the war just masked it until it eventually fizzled out in 1946.

Nevertheless, it was clear that the economy did experience a revitalization at the outset of the war, in part because a number of the old antiquated industries that had been shut down during the Depression such as steel mills and other construction markets fired back up again in order to supply soldiers with the needed equipment and armaments. As we've seen, this was also a time when the gender normative division of labor was being breached, and more and more women were entering the workforce. With the US and its connection to the war, this meant that many men ended up having to leave those jobs which were then filled by women, and at this time the unemployment rate was well below 10%, something that would have seemed unprecedented nearly a decade before.

Chapter 12 – Return to the Common Theme: War

Unfortunately for the world, the Great War was not the War to End All Wars. Another, this time, bloodier conflict erupted a mere twenty years later. The defeated Germany felt oppressed by the terms opposed by Woodrow Wilson and, with a resurgent leader, went on the offense again.

WORLD WAR II

Once again America was interested in a neutral position. A new addition to this war was the East Asian power of Japan. The Japanese, after having opened up to the West (mostly through American persuasion) in the early part of the century, wanted an empire of their own. Their imperial ventures in East Asian and the Pacific eventually led to inevitable conflict with America. Japan also happened to be allied with Germany, which put it on the opposite side of traditional American allies France and Britain. The Japanese were involved in WWI, but the empire took on more importance in this conflict.

Britain had pleaded with America to join the war, but America was not interested in committing more troops to another mechanized, highly efficient meat grinder. The official stance was Neutrality and avoiding "foreign entanglements." America signed a deal with Britain called the Destroyers for Bases Agreement, which saw America supporting Britain in the war indirectly. The United States shipped fifty destroyers were transferred to the British Navy from America and America was given rights to build and maintain bases in several territories claimed by the British Empire. A further agreement, named Lend-Lease, was a program by the United States to send food, oil, and materials, including weaponry, to Britain, France, China, and others, in exchange for leasing lands to build bases. This was not a direct involvement of the United States in the war, but it significantly helped the Allied powers against their enemies as they could rely on the natural resource reserves of the US and even sometimes armaments from the massive American industrial base.

The avoidance of entanglement in foreign wars, however, could not last forever. The same sentiment of non-involvement that had been espoused by citizens prior to the first World War was similar, but this time there was a sense of pride in the fact that they had managed to win that war and pull themselves out of the Depression. Also, the United States was now a global empire with global interests, and this necessitated their eventual role in what would follow. The imperial Japanese expansion in the Pacific came to a head with the Japanese attack on Pearl Harbor in Hawaii on December 7, 1941. The attack, sometimes known as Operation Z, was a surprise military attack on the naval base in Hawaii. Taken completely off guard, there was little that American soldiers could do and nearly 2400 were killed in what FDR would later say in his famous speech was "a day which will live in infamy". Some theorists have put forth ideas that the government knew about the attack but did not stop it in order to galvanize the public into joining the war on behalf of the Allies. This certainly corroborates with the fact that at the time many American citizens did not want to get involved and there was a feeling both in the societal and political realms that this time the US should stay out. After the attack on Pearl Harbor, any sort of public reservation about joining the war seemed to vanish.

Following the entry into the war, the United States joined the fray in the ever expanding war. The war saw a plethora of new technologies instituted, with the Germans having an early advantage in aircraft and encryption. The latter was a major motivator for the development of the computer, which would come to shape the world. A superweapon was born, as well.

Many German scientists, fleeing Nazi persecution, fled Germany to the United States. Many of these scientists then worked on a top secret project known as The Manhattan Project. The fruit of the project was the atomic bomb. While never used against Germany, the bomb was used against

Japan. Today it is still controversial whether the President should have authorized the use of the weapons, but history does not change. Two successful nuclear attacks against Japan forced the surrender of the Imperial Japanese military in 1945, and the United States emerged as the sole superpower. While Germany, the USSR, and Japan had all committed research to the atomic bomb, after the war in 1946 only the United States had the technology.

Britain, France, Germany, Japan, and the Soviet Union lay in ruins. The United States, on the other hands, was, just like the last European war, mostly unscathed except for its missing citizens who had died in the war. Its infrastructure was intact and the following years witnessed the final steps of the American Republic becoming a global force. The new superweapon, the atomic bomb, was not America's alone for long. In 1949 the Soviet Union, promoting communism, successfully tested its own nuclear weapon.

OPERATION PAPERCLIP

One major consequence of World War II was a buildup of technology. The warring powers spent great sums of money to counter each other's research. Germany did not go to war believing its technology was inferior to the Allies. In fact, the Blitzkrieg style of warfare, which handed the Germans quick victory, were made possible largely due to the technological Nazi supremacy. Similar technological superiority had given the colonists of early America a significant advantage over the Natives. If aliens invade any time soon, their technological superiority will make any human resistance meek.

For this reason, the United States and the Soviet Union, even before the end of the war, prepared to take in Nazi scientists who may have valuable information and research performed for the Third Reich. Operation Paperclip was such an initiative. The most prominent scientist to be recruited through the program was Werner von Braun.

Von Braun had helped Germany develop its V2 rockets which had rained terror upon Britain during the war. Instead of trying such scientists in courts or barring them from employment in the victorious Allied Nations, the US recruited them into working for the upcoming Cold War. The US knew the USSR was the only other nation on Earth at the time capable of challenging the US, and for that reason, the US embarked on a mission recruiting Nazi scientists before they could be captured or enticed by the Russians. Truman ordered that no scientist with Nazi ties be recruited, but that would have rendered ineligible most of the scientists expected to be recruited. For that reason, many of the scientists with Nazi backgrounds were given false biographies to allow them entry into the United States.

Von Braun helped bring the United States the rockets that would launch satellites and men into space during the Space Race. It was not just aerospace engineers that received offers, though. Chemists and physicists were among the scientists included in the recruitment. Overall, the United States and the United Kingdom brought in 1,600 scientists from the end of World War II to the end of the Cold War.

INTERNMENT CAMPS

At the time of going to war with Japan, the United States was actually home to many hundreds of thousands of Japanese immigrants. These were everyday citizens who had come to America in order to find a new life, and many were business owners who had built themselves from the ground up. With the US embroiled in a war with Japan though, certain racial fears began to surface. Racism and violence preceded a general sentiment of suspicion surrounding Japanese immigrants, 62% of them who were actually United States citizens. This would eventually lead to the creation of internment camps for all Japanese citizens in the country and for Roosevelt to institute Executive Order 9066 which effectively allowed the military at home to exclude all Japanese citizens on the entire west coast.

Internment camps were created, very similar to the sort of POW camps that soldiers overseas would experience, and were fenced off to prevent Japanese people from leaving. This came as a blow to American-Japanese people who had cut ties with their homeland and who had been living in the United States (sometimes for generations), and was indicative of how scared the general population was of the Japanese threat. The irony was that the majority of people interned were men, women, and children who had never held a weapon in their lives.

DEVELOPMENT OF NUCLEAR POWER

As war raged on two fronts for the United States – both in Europe and in the Indo-China sphere with Japan – it was clear that *this* war would become a much longer, more drawn out, and subsequently more costly war for everyone involved. In the final push into Normandy on D-Day the Allies had effectively gained a foothold in Europe again and pushed back Hitler's armies. It was only a matter of time now before Germany would eventually accept surrender. However, the war in the Pacific was still going strong, and much harder to end – part of the reason was because Japan was effectively isolated. On one side it had the entire breadth of the Pacific Ocean, on the other a number of countries in between it and the next Allied super power. An overland and terrestrial approach was deemed too expensive.

Around this time the Manhattan Project had already been underway in New Mexico. With brilliant minds like Oppenheimer on site, the scientists there had been experimenting with the power of nuclear fission in the form of atomic bombs. The first atomic bomb trial was on July 16, 1945, and the massive explosion that followed was enough to convince both the president and commanders that this was a weapon that could effectively end the war once and for all, avoiding protracted losses of life on both sides of the conflict. On August 6th a uranium gun-type bomb named "Little Boy" was dropped on the Japanese city of Hiroshima, leveling it in an explosion that vaporized thousands. Harry Truman, now president of the US, called for the surrender of Japan and three days later another bomb, "Fat Man", was dropped on Nagasaki with similar consequences. The loss of life is estimated to be as high as 146,000 in Hiroshima and 80,000 in Nagasaki, and in the months that followed a huge number of people became infected with radiation sickness

While the war had come to an end, the cost was felt most strongly by the Japanese people. The bombs had not been – like Pearl Harbor – a tactical or military target, but rather a pedestrian one, and the majority of those who died were everyday citizens. Today the ethical implications of using a nuclear bomb are still debated and questions still raised as to whether the US was justified in their actions. Currently, there is a war memorial in Hiroshima designed to foster peace in the hopes that nuclear war will never again be used as an incentive or solution in a world conflict.

COLD WAR, KOREA, and McCARTHYISM

The diametric difference between communism and capitalism, coupled with America not being the only power with nuclear technology, set off the Cold War. The fear of the spreading influence of Communism forced the United States into a position to "contain" the Soviet Union and its influence. The paranoia reached a fever pitch in the 1950s with McCarthyism, named after the Congressman who instigated the accusations. At the same time, the first proxy war between America and the USSR occurred.

The United States practiced an official policy of containment against the USSR to stem its spread. In 1950 the northern, communist forces attempted to take over the entire Korean Peninsula (which was under joint American and Soviet occupation following the partitioning of the Japanese Empire). This lead to a three-year, devastating war for Korea. The nation is still divided by the border set up by this conflict, over six decades since the beginning of the war and still decades after the fall of the USSR. The last two years were an attrition war that eventually drove enemy forces to the 38th parallel where a demilitarized zone was set up between North and South. Today it still exists, and is a source of grief for many in the South who still have family in the North.

The fear that communism could eventually take over the entire globe and extinguish the American way of life had some unexpected side effects. The political freedom and freedom of speech championed by Americans since the beginning of the nation (in one form or another) was hampered by the Red Scare or McCarthyism. During this era, 1950 to 1956, the Congressman Joseph McCarthy accused many and implemented investigations, but he was not the only one. Thousands of Americans were accused of sympathizing with communism, and while those sent to prison for espionage or other punishable crimes was relatively low, those thousands affected still lost jobs and faced social expulsion.

Simply being accused or investigated could substantiate the removal from a position, and many faced being fired from their jobs for such investigations. The feverish pursuit of suspected communist sympathizers showed signs of the suspension of "innocent until proven guilty." While that did not hold up in court, it still meant people were unable to find employment afterwards. One of the most notorious and well-known examples of this is the Blacklist in Hollywood, where applicants were denied employment for suspected communist sympathies. The movement was not supported by the entire populace, and even Truman, who was not particularly liberal, criticized the actions as "in a free country, we punish men for the crimes they commit, but never for the opinions they have." Of course, to make an opinion a crime only requires an act of legislation, but there was no such law at the time.

One of the effects of this Red Scare and the increasing paranoia supplied by McCarythism was a reboot of the old Federal Bureau of Investigation. It suddenly became focal point, involved in a number of investigations, and grew considerably during these years. Under the auspices of Edgar

J. Hoover who became the Director of the FBI, whole task forces were sent out to question those with supposed Communist affiliations – this led to thousands of people being interrogated. However, Hoover was adamant about not revealing his sources or informants, so often times people had no way of controverting the evidence placed against them or even knowing who had accused them. This practice would eventually come to define the late 1950's and McCarthy's name would become synonymous down the line with paranoia, questioning loyalty, and poor reasoning, a legacy that he probably had no intention of leaving behind.

With increased hostilities between Russia, the Cold War did not end quickly, but following WWII neither side was prepared for a full-out conflict.. Immediately following the Red Scare, the Soviet Union put its first satellite into space, and the United States responded with its Space Program. The possibility that ideology could beat Western capitalism in technology caused significant anxiety among the population, especially when it seemed whoever controlled space could quickly deliver nuclear weapons while rendering the other side's weapons obsolete. As with many aspects of American history, and indeed history in general, the Space Race was driven by military dominance and security issues.

Fun Fact:

The Korean War, although it managed to produce a division between North and South, was one war in which the United States never actually signed a peace treaty after the conclusion of hostilities. Although there is a peace treaty with the democratic South, a peace treaty or ceasefire has never been signed with North Korea – meaning that for all intents and purposes, the US is still at war with them, six decades later.

Chapter 13 – The Space Race

On October 4, 1957, the Soviet Union launched Sputnik I into orbit; it was the very first time in history for such a feat, which served as the spark that started the Space Race. A few months after, the Russians sent another satellite into orbit, the Sputnik II, and this time it carried a living payload, Laika, the dog. This struck another cord in the ego of the United States.

Not to be outdone by their Cold War rival, on 1961, the United States and then President John F. Kennedy announced that they would be increasing funding for space exploration, and made a hefty promise that before the decade ends they will be sending a man on the moon. Sadly, JFK would not live to see the fruits of his labor; on November 22, 1963, an assassin's bullet would take away the President's life. Lyndon Johnson, Kennedy's VP, would take over the office and continue his dream of sending a man to the moon.

On October 1, 1958, the US government formed the National Aeronautics and Space Administration (NASA) to replace the National Advisory Committee on Aeronautics (NACA), which then led to serious studies on how they could send people into outer space.

In 1959, the Soviet space program seemingly got a leg up over its American counterpart by launching the Luna 2, the first space probe to actually land on the moon. Then, on April 1961, they successfully sent cosmonaut Yuri Gagarin into orbit and got him back home safely. On May 5 at that same year, the Americans finally sent their own astronaut, Alan Shepard, into outer space. However, Shepard did not orbit the earth like what Gagarin did.

Space race casualties

The Space Race, as flamboyant and entertaining as it was, was not without incident. A couple of serious setbacks on both sides of the Space Race almost halted their efforts. For instance, on the Soviet side, Sergey Korolyov, the chief engineer of their space program, suddenly died and left a vacuum in their organization. It took years before the Soviet space program could find a suitable replacement and continue their research. To make matters worse, cosmonaut Vladimir Komarov, died because the parachute of his Soyuz I space capsule failed to deploy upon re-entry into the atmosphere; reports back then said that he was "crying in rage" as he plummeted to his demise.

On the other hand, a horrifying accident almost turned off the US public to the prospect of continuing with the Space Race. Astronauts Virgil "Gus" Grissom, Roger Chaffee, and Ed White were conducting a launch pad test on the Apollo 1 when a fire suddenly burst out inside the spacecraft; all three men died that day. NASA, in respect to the deaths of the three astronauts, decided to slow down their space exploration research so they could concentrate more on the safety and well-being of the crew.

The culmination of the space race

On July 16, 1969, American astronauts Neil Armstrong, Edwin "Buzz" Aldrin, and Michael Collins, launched from Cape Canaveral onboard the Apollo 11 spacecraft. After four days, their landing craft successfully touched down on the surface of the moon, and Neil Armstrong then became the first man to step on the moon, and he said that it was "one small step for man, one giant leap for mankind." With this, the United States officially won the space race, and actually fulfilled Kennedy's promise that they would be sending a man to the moon before the end of the 1960's.

The Apollo program also represented a shift in the American psyche. Suddenly it was possible to do anything, and this sense of national pride would resonate for decades to come. It was also one of the most expensive programs ever funded by the US, an estimated $20 billion – today, with inflation taken into account, that would have been equal to around $206 billion.

The new Saturn style engines were much larger than the sorts used in previous flights, and a huge amount of technological prowess went into the project. This, more than anything, is what the program really meant as a legacy for future space travel: it pushed the envelope in terms of what had up until then even been dreamed of, and the entire nation tuned into the NASA broadcast when they stepped onto the moon.

This successful mission to the moon would bolster support for NASA, and soon other space attempts would be made including the creation of Skylab, the first and only independently built spacecraft by the US. Much later it would also give birth to the Space Shuttle program which would send up numerous space craft and increase our understanding of the universe beyond the atmosphere. Every subsequent satellite we have sent into the darkness owes its existence to the adventure and sense of wonder that was exercised back in the 1960's – and today, the most modern incarnations, including the Mars Rover and the International Space Station, are representative not only of the Unite States role in this endeavor, but in a global effort to expand our knowledge and our bounds.

Fun facts:

Space Race veteran Alan Shepard was the fifth man to walk on the moon, but he was the first to play sports on the lunar surface. After landing the Apollo 14 lander in what was the most accurate one in NASA's history thus far, he then proceeded to hit two golf balls. The second one, Shepard said, travelled for miles.

The one thing that surprised many of the astronauts that walked on the moon was not the captivating beauty of the landscape, but rather they were taken aback by the smells; in other words, the moon stinks (it has been likened to the burned smell of gunpowder).

This is one "not-so-fun" fact. Even though the Soviet Union claimed that Laika, the dog that was on the Sputnik II, survived for almost a week in orbit, some reports said that the poor dog only managed to live for a couple of hours and died because the cabin got too hot.

Chapter 14 – Nixon and the Watergate Scandal

Richard Milhous Nixon was quite the president. During his first term, Nixon presided over the Apollo 11 space mission, which invariably finished the Space Race between the USA and the Soviet Union, and he also ended American involvement in the Vietnam War and ended the military draft practice. He was so good at the job that he got re-elected in one of the largest landslide victories in the history of the US. However, things started to unravel for President Nixon in the 70s.

Before the fall

Richard Milhous Nixon actually had a lot of achievements under his belt even before he became president for the first time. He was on active duty in the Navy Reserve during World War II. His rabid pursuit of the Hiss case (where an American government official was accused of being a Soviet spy) cemented his reputation for being anti-communist and thereby gaining prominence among the American people. With the atmosphere in the United States reflected in McCarythism and a sense of trying to unify the country against a singular (and often times vaguely obscured) threat, it was the perfect environment for a Republican such as Nixon to gain support.

Despite narrowly losing the presidential race to John F. Kennedy in 1960 and losing the Californian gubernatorial race to Pat Brown in 1962, Nixon still tried to run for the top office in 1968, and he finally won after he defeated Hubert Humphrey.

Discovery and conviction

In 1972, five people were arrested when they broke into the Democratic National Committee's headquarters at the Watergate office complex in the Capital. It turned out that the burglars actually had ties to the CIA and other government agencies, and that they were sent there to plant microphones and steal confidential documents. The Democrats suspected that Nixon had a hand in the break in, but they had no hard evidence that linked him to the crime.

After some time had passed, a mysterious informant with the codename "Deepthroat" surfaced, and he/she knew that Nixon did have a hand at the Watergate break in, and what's more he also employed other dirty and illegal tactics against his political opponents. Deepthroat, who would later be identified as Mark Felt of the FBI, actually provided solid evidence linking Nixon to the Watergate scandal, which prompted Congress to investigate. In the midst of the investigation of Watergate, numerous other politicians and government officials received indictments for their involvement. Public outcry led to multiple impeachment claims and calls for Nixon's resignation. In spite of losing support from the Democratic side, and even from his own party, Nixon denied any wrongdoing on his behalf or any knowledge of the break-in.

It all came to a head when the impeachment hearings got hold of a tape – very famously referred to as the 'Smoking gun Tape' – which proved Nixon knew of the break-in to bug an opponent's office and had actively encouraged attempts to thwart the investigation. It was the last nail in the coffin and after more than a year of public indignation, Nixon resigned from his post as the President of the United States.

Did Nixon get convicted for the Watergate Scandal?

No. When Gerald Ford took over the reins of the presidency after Nixon resigned, he granted the former president a presidential pardon, which means that Nixon gained immunity for the crimes that he was supposed to be tried for.

Nixon's reputation never really recovered after Watergate. His fall from grace was so abrupt; one year he was the darling of the people, and the following one he was the devil incarnate. Until now, when you ask people who they think was the worst president in US history, they would most likely say it was Nixon.

Ever since Watergate, every national scandal that would surface would almost always have "-gate" suffixed to it.

Chapter 15 – End of the Cold War and Pax Americana

The 1980s witnessed various events pertaining to the Cold War. Surely the ideological war between the world's only two superpowers would influence the world, and the United States was one of those superpowers. One way the United States pressured the Soviet Union was through spending, as the Soviet economy was much weaker than the United States.

MAD AND THE STRATEGIC DEFENSE INITIATIVE

The doctrine of mutually assured destruction (MAD) formed the basis of the US-Soviet relationship for most of the Cold War. The concept claimed that a nuclear nation would not attack another as it would certainly receive retaliatory strikes against its own lands. The concept may have indeed been a mad one, but it kept nuclear war from ever breaking out. The US President Reagan, however, was not a proponent of the scheme and wanted to implement a defensive doctrine as well. His plan was the Strategic Defense Initiative (SDI).

The defense included land and space based methods to eliminate the Soviet threat. Many critics of the initiative feared it would destabilize the delicate balance afforded by MAD, or Mutually Assured Destruction, the thought that if both powers did go to power with nuclear weapons, it wouldn't matter who shot first because both sides would effectively annihilate each other. If the Soviets were suddenly disabled from attacking the US because of defense, the offensive MAD doctrine would no longer apply. That would make the Soviet Union vulnerable to an American attack without the deterrent of a return strike. Many thought this would force the Soviets to act preemptively and start a nuclear war. Furthermore, the futuristic style of the initiative resulted in being nicknamed the Star Wars defense. This program actually was built by Reagan as an *alternative* to the MAD paradigm, and was his attempt at trying to overhaul the strategy of nuclear deterrence into one that was more aggressive.

While the Star Wars program (so called after George Lucas' Star Wars movie because of its use of lasers) did not ever gain much traction under his term of office, it and other programs implemented by Reagan forced the Soviet Union to spend heavily in military research, and this is partially credited with the fall of the USSR. Later, when Bill Clinton would finally enter into office, the program would be overhauled again, this time turned into the Ballistic Missile Defense Organization (or BMDO) and, like the name suggested, its interests more heavily focused on defense of a possible missile attack. Elements of Reagan's old SDI program is still relevant in today's military research, and there is even a plan to institute a laser based defense system around 2020.

END OF THE USSR AND THE BEGINNING OF GLOBAL AMERICAN DOMINANCE

The crumbling of the Berlin Wall in 1989 foreshadowed the crumbling of the Soviet Union in the coming years. The void left behind was less dangerous than it could have been. The extensive stockpile of nuclear weapons in Russia and other former Soviet states remained surprisingly protected and, while the general population suffered from extreme hardship, the weapons were not sold off or misplaced during the ensuing chaos.

Once the USSR was dissolved, there was no longer a challenger to American power. The old powers of Europe had long ago ceased to play such a central role as their offspring, America. Russia was a husk of its former glory as the USSR. China was nowhere near as industrialized as it currently is, and the European Union, even today, cannot muster hard power like the United States – sometimes it cannot even keep its own members, as Brexit demonstrated. This military dominance has given way to an Americanization of the globe.

The United States became the sole power at a time when the globe was becoming increasingly connected. Today the world is highly interconnected through trade, finance, and communication. The Internet, the rise of which is nothing short of a Revolution, instantly connects people from all over the world. Although the Internet was not as widespread in the 1990s as it is today, American culture was still exported en masse to the rest of the world. Entertainment, consumerism, advertising, and American-style democracy has been exported to nations the world over, and without the end of the Cold War, this development would never have taken place.

The relative peace through the world following the end of the Cold War was nicknamed Pax Americana (after the similar peace throughout the Roman world when Rome controlled much of Europe and North Africa). The United States worked to democratize various nations and incorporate such nations into the global economic system. The result is the modern, globalized world. There were still wars, even within the borders of largely peaceful Europe, but they have not been on the scale of previous wars, especially the World Wars.

That said, the geopolitical spectrum in regards to the US took a very drastic turn on September 11, 2001 when a terrorist attack involving two planes ended up bringing down the World Trade Centers in New York. This attack, carried out by members of Al-Qaeda, had the effect of suddenly humbling the US again – in much the same way that Pearl Harbor brought the US out of its insulated world perspective, so too did 9/11 come as a reminder that there was a great amount of strife and political conflict outside their borders, and the terrorist attack on one of the primary capitals and symbols of America's values could not be understated in the effects it had. Security in general increased amazingly as people felt they were no longer safe, and this prompted a number of incursions and military campaigns, especially in Iraq and Afghanistan.

At home though globalization has led to the loss of many economic opportunities for Americans which were once the backbone of the American economy. The 2008 housing bubble crisis became a huge source of interference in the economy, and though it was labeled only as a recession, it had a similar effect to the Great Depression in that many people lost their jobs. This prompted a movement in the US to disparage big banks that were 'too big to fail', and was the catalyst for the Occupy Wall Street movement which, although it lost steam, cemented itself in the cultural milieu as a significant issue. Additionally, industry and manufacturing, which had catapulted the United States to the forefront of global economics in the early part of the 20th century, started to migrate to lower-wage countries in East and South East Asia. The major power likely to challenge America in the future, China, arose from the ashes of Japanese rule and decades of the brutal communist rule to become the world's manufacturer. Others have chipped away at sectors once dominated by America, such as automobiles and steel. The world is becoming more multipolar instead of bipolar or monopolar (the US as the only superpower).

However, American influence is still widely felt, and global newspapers are more likely to talk about American politics than American newspapers are to report on foreign politics. The United States still maintains a dominant position in technology, and the country knows retaining that position is essential to maintain global dominance. Cultural, American music and film are still widely enjoyed throughout the globe, and the country's central position has given it the ability to spread its language – the American spread is a continuation of the British Empire's language's influence in the world. The world uses English as its medium of communication, and the United States was in the right position at the right time to capitalize on the changes enveloping the planet.

In the 2010s, the multipolar world continues to show signs of strain and the Pax Americana has fractured. The wars in Syria, Afghanistan, and Iraq have destabilized already contentious areas. The United States suffered its worst attack on its own soil since Pearl Harbor in 2001 and has since been on a quest to rid the world of terrorism. Moreover, state actors have started to conduct cyber intrusions, and the new front will emerge from the same medium that allowed America to spread its influence into every home and hand.

Fun Fact:

Regarding the belief technology is all-important to security and dominance, it was illegal to export encryption from the United States until the 1990s. Having seen the role encryption played in World War II and the Cold War, the United States classified encryption under the munitions codes, because it could be used as a weapon. Only in the 1990s and the spread of the Internet did it become legal to export it. The encryption we all use every day for secure communication over the Internet was, at one point, not permitted as a technological export.

Chapter 16 – The United States Constitution

Although the original United States Constitution came into effect way back in 1789 we include it here as the last chapter because it has been a continually changing and organic document, and a pivotal instrument in terms of the way it's shaped the United States up to the present day. The Constitution experienced its first draft way back during the beginning of the Americas when the country was still new and the provisional government still in the process of attempting to put together a system of laws and government that would last for centuries. It wasn't until 1788 that the Constitution in its more or less complete form was finally submitted to Congress – who were responsible for the very long and wearisome process of ratification.

One of the major constituent articles of the Constitution was based on the Magna Carta and strove to give rights to everyone in America as citizens. There was also, according to both Locke and Hobbes (popular philosophers and social critics of the age), several provisions put in, and these became the backbone of the Constitution and, indeed, the overall American sense of nationalism. These happened to fall into three categories of a social contract that the government was supposed to protect and included the basic rights to life, liberty, and freedom. Then, in 1791 another set of 10 laws were added and these included the Bill of Rights, further guarantees for all the members of the US that helped to stabilize a sort of moral compass in the populace.

Article One in the Constitution described what the Congress would be in the United States and all the other legislative branches, and set down a list of responsibilities and rules for them to follow.

Article Two involved paragraphs that were designed to give the President the power of the military strength of his nation and militia, and has been a staple of policy ever since, and something that is often brought up in American politics and elections that "the President has his finger on the launch codes", referring to the capacity for a President to control the nuclear arsenal. It primarily deals with the office of the President, and contains provisions related to what happens if he is impeached.

Article Three has to do with the court system and lists out ad nauseam all the different laws associated with jurisdiction. It is interesting to note that this article also contains the definition of treason and how to handle it, and that treasonous thoughts alone are not an indictable offense but must include 'overt' actions.

Article Four is all about how states get along with other states and how legislated state laws and federal laws interact with one another. This was important because one clause prevented the Federal Government from favoring one state over another, and made it so that all states had to be regarded equally in the eyes of the government. It also included clauses about extradition from one state to another. Although this is not much of an issue these days, even though states do have their own laws, back in the day crossing from one state to another was a costly and bureaucratic nightmare.

Article Five is a very important element because it is what outlines the process for attempting to amend the Constitution. This is of note because as we've seen the Constitution is a very fluid dynamic that has changed over the years to reflect the common values and principles of the age, and this is a vital factor not only in the process of democracy, but in helping to modernize our approach to living. Laws that do not make sense or harm the values or US, such as Prohibition, are capable of being repealed, and it is this flexibility that has helped to shape the US into what it is today. As a side note, it should also be observed that Article Four is what allows Congress to pass new amendments, and that in 1808 when it first had the power to do so attempted to legislate ratification for a ban on slavery – a decision that helped to establish the American ideal of liberty.

Article Six and the last one in the Constitution outlines the process and rules relating to the outline of creating their new kind of government. One has to remember that back then before the United States were *truly* united, there were a number of states, especially in the south, that resisted integration into the grand design of the United States of America, and Article Six was crafted in such a way as to bring these states into the fold.

The Constitution has had 27 amendments made to it since its inception, and other than the Bill of Rights these include safeguard of liberty and justice designed to ensure that the Federal Government would assist states in trouble, other bills guaranteeing rights and privileges, and a number of safeguards to civil rights. The most recent amendment (27) came about in 1992 to prevent members of government from giving themselves pay raises.

While the Constitution stands as a blazing example of contemporary democratic thought, there have been a number of criticism leveled at it, the first being that in its original form it did not specify who and who did not have the right to vote. This would become an issue later down the road during the Civil Rights Movements and Women's Suffrage Movements when black minorities and women groups would rise up and demand the ability to vote and participate in the political affairs of the United States.

Both periods were very difficult, especially for minorities, and because men had dominated the powerful roles up until then. Their eventual success in not only getting the right to vote but laying the foundation for increased representation across the board has continued to this day and acts a reminder of the American spirit to endure, and that we still have a long way to go before we can say we are a truly a country of equals.

[76]

Fun Fact:

While only 27 amendments have been passed and officially ratified and recognized, there are a number of amendments that are still pending, some going as far back as 1922 including a Child Labor law that would limit and restrict jobs for those under 18 years of age.

A number of other amendments were put forward but rejected, the most prominent being the Equal Rights Amendment of 1972. Had it been passed, it would have prohibited discrimination and deprivation of rights by the state or Federal institutions based on sex. Unfortunately the proposal failed by three votes, and was never brought forward again. Another interesting one that failed was a proposal to give the District of Columbia the ability to vote and have full representation in the Senate, effectively making it another State.

Chapter 17 – Political Parties

Political parties in the United States have undergone numerous changes through the years, but in general the goals of each was to establish a democracy that helped everyone and would see to the interests of all citizens. In general, there were usually two main parties, a form of government that has come to be known as bipartisan. Nevertheless, there have been plenty of historical parties in the past, and we'll take a look at them and at the current form of government.

The Toleration Party was started back in 1801 and has actually held power to the present day, though it was heavily weakened by the War of 1812 when the Federalist perspectives it held dear began to decline. They were also once affiliated with the Democratic-Republican Party.

The Anti-Masonic Party came about in regards to what they feared was an excess of Freemasonry, especially in the higher echelons of government (recall that a number of the founding fathers had Masonic ties). They came to power and only lasted a little over a decade, allying themselves at one point with the Whigs, but they did manage to introduce some significant changes in government such as the idea of party platforms, which is still an element of political discourse today. It was also the first ever third party to be created within the US.

The Nullifier Party had as their goal the ability to 'nullify' federal law within states. This would have given more power to regional lawmakers, and as the party was founded in South Carolina it would come as no surprise that they wanted to try and separate themselves from government intervention during the 1800's.

The Boston Tea Party was a relatively recent political party that was only disbanded in 2012. They were primarily advertised as a libertarian party and thought that the government should be more active in all levels in order to best serve the citizenry. They were also quite active in attempting to convince the US to withdraw troops from both enemy and allied territories, and were one of the only parties to call for an investigation into the events of 9/11.

Current Political Parties

In terms of political parties that are current and active, they are most prominently the bipartisan communities of the Republican and Democratic parties. The Republican side is often called the GOP (for Grand Old Party) and is a very conservative right-wing party that favors a lot of the traditional values in the United States, including the right to bear arms, military expansion and industrial expansion, and the traditional definitions of marriage and life, which has led to conflict in a number of social and legal spheres involving abortion, same-sex marriages, LGBT soldiers and the military's treatment of them, and issues related to death penalties and physician assisted suicide. They also have generally strong libertarian economic ideals and are social conservatives in comparison to their Democratic opposition. There is also a trend in those who support the Republican Party to be more spread out in terms of geographic location, especially in rural areas. While the Presidents past and present have all espoused a religious stance, it has also been considerably more overt among Conservatives, including George Bush and runner-up Mitt Romney who lost the election to Barack Obama.

In contrast, the Democratic Party actually traces back to Jefferson and the Democratic-Republic Party, and was originally a form of classic liberalism. Nowadays they are a bit more moderate, but still focus on trends of equality, both socially and economically, and this includes advocating for welfare, something that Republicans tend to oppose. They also encourage labor unions and social programs, and generally take a more involved role in politics and the economic makeup of a country, again in contrast to Republicans who tend to favor a more individualist capitalist-driven worldview. Historically they were huge supporters of the New Deal because this was one of the first times that the government had both a strong and direct influence in the labor market and that the economy had been geared toward trying to ensure equality. In general, the Democratic Party has also been associated with more socially conscious approaches to government and daily life which has included support for same-sex marriages and abortions, opposition to torture and regulation on gun control, and a strong emphasis on immigration and making it easier to gain citizenship. Politically, they support cutting some funding to the military expenditures and imposing carbon taxes, while the Conservative leadership generally opposes this in favor of keeping industry active. As a result of all of this, many minorities are often attracted to the Democratic perspective because it is more inclusive.

There is also an Independent category in the current American government and this is usually held by someone who does not fit wholly the policies or beliefs of either the Democrats or the Republicans. That said, many of them often do share certain loyalties to one party or another. In the most recent election this was demonstrated by Bernie Sanders who was running on his own platform that was geared toward a more leftist interpretation of Democratic thought.

These also include some lesser known parties that include the Green Party. In the States this is a very progressive far-left party that has a number of views similar to the Democratic Party, but are far from moderate. They have a very strong ecological and environmentally friendly stance, and advocate for grass-roots democracy. This is in contrast to the major political parties who prefer a very centralized form of governing – for the Greens, decentralized government and economic policies are considered more beneficial, not only in terms of stabilizing and maintain said economies but also in giving freedom to citizen. They are also huge proponents of social and equal rights including a women's right to choose, nonviolence, global justice, and women's rights in general.

[80]

The other main independent party currently is the Libertarian Party, which is more like the classical liberals from several hundred years ago. A number of their policies include the fact that they support laissez-faire economics, and want to abolish welfare – in many ways they have conservative views on a number of issues, thinking that capitalism is both good and should be exercised, and that the state does not have an obligation or responsibility to 'bail out' banks or individuals. On the other hand they also list abolishing the IRS and gold standard, lowering taxes, and allowing people to opt out of their Social Security, thereby decreasing the influence that the Federal government would have in the lives of the populace. Like the Greens and Democrats they also have strong views on eradicating the death penalty and supporting same-sex marriages. An interesting fact about the Libertarian Party is that they were the first party to cast an electoral vote for a woman.

Conclusion

These are just some of the most important events that molded the United States of America to what it is today. As you have probably noticed, not everything that the US ventured into was always a success; there were a couple of times in its colorful history when it actually made a couple of serious mistakes that could have spelled into massive disasters. But one of the primary goals of history is to learn from the past so as to avoid those errors of judgement in the future, as the old credo suggests: "Those who fail to learn the lessons of history are doomed to repeat them." Indeed, there have been many ups and downs in American history, and what we can see when we stand back and look at events objectively is that despite tragedies that have occurred (the subjugation of blacks, genocide of Native Americans, repression of women) there have also been numerous positive aspects as well such as exploration and inventions right up to the pivotal events of walking on the moon.

In a sense, this is the role of history, to provide us a context with which we might approach our present and understand our own place in it. The coming years will present America with many challenges, but the American people have always found a way through. No conflict on the scale of the Civil War is imminent in American history, and no outside threat seems persistent or powerful enough to bring the American juggernaut down. Nevertheless, we must always exercise caution and humility. The variables that determine each and every event in history are sometimes hard to understand, and therefore vigilance is the price we must pay.

Reading about these events, be it positive or negative, only shows just how persistent and optimistic the American people really are. I hope you enjoyed reading this short overview of American history, and that it has inspired you to learn more.

Printed in Great Britain
by Amazon